From Dream to Reality:Business ventures, values, and making a long-term impact

Joseph L. Santos

INTRODUCTION

NAVIGATING THE PATH OF INNOVATION

In the realm of innovation, where groundbreaking ideas redefine industries and shape the future, the power of singular thinking emerges as a guiding force. It is the beacon that illuminates the path less traveled, leading to uncharted territories where creativity thrives and transformative concepts take root. This exploration delves into the profound impact of singular thinking, revealing how it propels visionaries from zero to one, enabling them to forge new frontiers and leave an indelible mark on the world.

The Essence Of Singular Thinking

At its core, singular thinking is the audacious act of challenging the status quo, of questioning norms that have long been accepted, and of envisioning what others perceive as impossible. It's the ability to detach from conventional thought patterns and to embark on a journey of unbounded imagination. Singular thinkers are not bound by the constraints of what "should" be; they're captivated by what "could" be.

Breaking Free From Conformity

Conformity is the enemy of innovation. It breeds a culture of sameness, where ideas become recycled and progress stagnates. Singular thinkers shatter these chains of conformity, unapologetically bringing their unique perspectives to the table. They recognize that the most revolutionary ideas often lie at the fringes of conventional thought. In this willingness to be unconventional, singular thinkers pave the way for new paradigms to emerge.

Questioning Assumptions

Singular thinkers are skilled questioners. They challenge assumptions that are so deeply ingrained in society's fabric that they go unnoticed by the masses. They ask why certain processes exist, why certain problems persist, and why certain solutions are considered viable. This relentless interrogation of the status quo enables them to identify gaps that others overlook, leading to breakthrough insights and innovative solutions.

Drawing Inspiration From Diverse Sources

The power of singular thinking is augmented by the ability to draw inspiration from disparate sources. Singular thinkers recognize that creativity flourishes when ideas from seemingly unrelated domains converge. The intersection of arts and sciences, technology and philosophy, and cultures and traditions can spark a fire of innovation that transcends boundaries. It's at these intersections that novel connections are made, birthing concepts that challenge convention.

The Courage To Be Different
Singular thinking requires immense courage. It's not easy to stand alone in a sea of conformity, to advocate for an idea that seems radical or unorthodox. Yet, it's this very courage that distinguishes innovators from the masses. They're willing to endure skepticism, doubt, and even ridicule in pursuit of their vision. Their unwavering commitment to their ideas empowers them to weather storms and emerge victorious.

The Dance With Uncertainty
Innovation thrives in the realm of uncertainty.
Singular thinkers embrace this uncertainty,
seeing it not as a hindrance, but as an
opportunity. They understand that exploring
the unknown is where true discovery lies.
This comfort with ambiguity allows them to
navigate uncharted waters with grace,
unburdened by the need for a clear roadmap.

Cultivating Singular Thinking
While singular thinking is often portrayed as
a rare and elusive trait, it can be cultivated
and nurtured. It begins with developing a
growth mindset - one that embraces
challenges and views failures as learning
opportunities. Curiosity is another key
element; a relentless curiosity about the
world and a thirst for knowledge fuel the
fires of singular thinking. Surrounding
oneself with diverse perspectives, engaging
in cross-disciplinary exploration, and

practicing open-mindedness all contribute to honing this transformative skill.

Singular Thinking In Action
History is replete with examples of singular thinking in action. Innovations like the internet, electric cars, and space travel were once considered far-fetched dreams. Yet, singular thinkers dared to challenge the norms of their time and pursued their visions with unwavering determination. These visionaries - from Steve Jobs to Elon Musk, Marie Curie to Nikola Tesla - defied convention and harnessed the power of singular thinking to shape the world as we know it today.

The Legacy OF Singular Thinking
The legacy of singular thinking extends beyond the innovations themselves. It serves as an inspiration to future generations of visionaries, igniting the spark of creativity in

minds eager to challenge the boundaries of what's possible. As each new wave of singular thinkers emerges, the cycle of innovation perpetuates, propelling humanity toward ever greater heights of progress and discovery.

The power of singular thinking is a force that propels humanity from the unknown to the known, from zero to one. It is a testament to the boundless potential of the human mind and its ability to reshape reality. From questioning assumptions to embracing uncertainty, from defying conformity to drawing inspiration from diverse sources, singular thinking is the compass that guides innovators on their transformative journeys. As we embrace this power, we tap into the wellspring of creativity that resides within us, and in doing so, we pave the way for a future marked by innovation, progress, and the relentless pursuit of what's possible.

ONE

THE POWER OF SINGULAR THINKING

In the development domain, where weighty thoughts reclassify enterprises and shape the future, the force of particular Reasoning arises as a directing power. The signal enlightens the way more unfamiliar, prompting strange regions where imagination flourishes, and extraordinary ideas flourish. This investigation dives into the significant effect of solitary Reasoning, uncovering how it moves visionaries from zero to one, empowering them to manufacture new wildernesses and make history.

The Pith OF Solitary Reasoning

At its center, particular Reasoning is the bold demonstration of rocking the boat, addressing standards that have been acknowledged for some time, and imagining what others see as unthinkable. It's the capacity to disconnect from ordinary idea designs and to set out on an excursion of the unbounded creative mind.

Particular scholars are not limited by what "ought to" be; they're dazzled by what "could" be.

Breaking Liberated From Congruity

Congruity is the foe of development. It breeds a culture of similarity, where thoughts become reused, and progress deteriorates. Solitary scholars break these chains of congruity, proudly offering their unique points of view that would be useful. They perceive that the most progressive thoughts frequently lie at the edges of ordinary ideas. In this readiness to be unusual, particular scholars prepare for new standards to arise.

Addressing Suspicions

Particular scholars are talented examiners. They challenge suspicions that are so profoundly imbued in the public eye's texture that they slip by everyone's notice by the majority. They inquire why certain cycles exist, why specific issues continue, and why certain arrangements are considered practical. This determined cross-examination of the norm empowers them to distinguish holes others ignore, prompting advancement experiences and imaginative arrangements.

Drawing Motivation From Assorted Sources

The force of solitary Reasoning is increased by the capacity to draw motivation from unique sources. Isolated scholars perceive that innovativeness thrives when thoughts from apparently inconsequential areas meet. The crossing point of expressions and sciences, innovation and Reasoning, and societies and customs can ignite a fire of development that rises above limits. At these convergences, original associations are made, birthing ideas that challenge the show.

The Mental Fortitude To Appear As Something Else

Particular Reasoning requires tremendous boldness. It's challenging to remain solitary in an ocean of congruity, to advocate for a thought that appears to be extremist or irregular. However, it's this very fortitude that recognizes trendsetters from the majority. They're willing to persevere through wariness, uncertainty, and even criticism in the quest for their vision. Their resolute obligation to their thoughts enables them to weather conditions and storms and arise successfully.

The Hit The Dance Floor With Vulnerability

Development flourishes in the domain of Vulnerability. Solitary masterminds embrace this Vulnerability, seeing it not as a prevention but as an open door. They comprehend that investigating the obscure is where genuine revelation lies. This solace with vagueness permits them to explore unknown waters with elegance, unburdened by the requirement for a reasonable guide.

Developing Particular Reasoning

While particular Reasoning is often depicted as an uncommon and tricky characteristic, it tends to be developed and sustained. It starts with fostering a development mentality that embraces difficulties and perspectives and disappointments as learning opens doors. Interest is one more critical component; a tenacious interest in the planet and a hunger for information fuel the flames of particular Reasoning. Encircling oneself with different viewpoints, participating in the cross-disciplinary investigation, and rehearsing liberality all increase this groundbreaking ability.

Particular Reasoning In Real Life

History is loaded with instances of particular Reasoning in real life. Advancements like the web, electric vehicles, and space travel were once viewed as unrealistic dreams. However, solitary masterminds thought for even a second to challenge the standards of their time and sought after their goals with steadfast assurance. These visionaries - from Steve Occupations to Elon Musk, Marie Curie to Nikola Tesla - opposed show and bridled the force of particular Reasoning to shape the world as far as we might be concerned today.

The Tradition Of Solitary Reasoning
The tradition of solitary Reasoning stretches out past the actual developments. It fills in as a motivation to people in the future of visionaries, lighting the flash of imagination in minds anxious to challenge the limits of what's conceivable. As each new rush of solitary masterminds arises, the development

pattern sustains, impelling humankind toward ever more noteworthy levels of progress and disclosure.

The force of solitary Reasoning is a power that compels humankind from the obscure to the known, from zero to one. It demonstrates the unfathomable capability of the human brain and its capacity to reshape reality. From addressing suspicions to embracing Vulnerability, from opposing adjustment to drawing motivation from assorted sources, solitary Reasoning is the compass that guides trendsetters on their extraordinary excursions. As we embrace this power, we tap into the wellspring of imagination that dwells inside us, and in doing as such, we prepare for a future set apart by development, progress, and the determined quest for what's conceivable.

TWO

IDENTIFYING AND CULTIVATING BREAKTHROUGH IDEAS

In the realm of advancement, advancement thoughts are the backbone of progress. They are the seeds from which extraordinary items, advances, and ideas develop, reshaping ventures and pushing the limits of human accomplishment. This investigation dives into the method involved with recognizing and developing these advanced thoughts, uncovering the systems, mentalities, and conditions that encourage development and drive the excursion from zero to one.

The Journey For Advanced Thoughts

Advancement thoughts can disturb, to challenge standards, and to make additional opportunities where none existed previously. They don't simply take care of existing issues; they imagine a world that is generally unique. This journey starts with the readiness to step past the natural, to address suspicions, and embrace the unexplored world. It's an excursion powered by interest, daringness and a persistent quest for the unprecedented.

Sustaining A Prolific Mentality

At the core of recognizing advancement thoughts lies a rich mentality. This outlook includes developing a profound feeling of interest, receptiveness, and a refusal to make due with unremarkableness. Advancement thoughts frequently rise up out of the transaction of different information and encounters. The individuals who search out new points of view, who draw in with changed disciplines, and who permit themselves to be animated by surprising sources are bound to find the seeds of development coincidentally.

Dissolving Limits
Advancement thoughts flourish in conditions where limits are broken down, and conventional storehouses are destroyed. The unbending detachment of disciplines smothers inventiveness; forward leaps happen at the crossing points of apparently inconsequential fields. Cooperative spaces, interdisciplinary activities, and stages that work with the cross-fertilization of thoughts

make fruitful ground for the rise of extraordinary ideas.

Sympathy And Client Centricity

Understanding the requirements and wants of clients is significant to distinguishing advancement thoughts. Sympathy permits trend-setters to see past their viewpoints and to associate with the difficulties looked at by others profoundly. By putting the client at the focal point of their inventive flow, trailblazers can uncover neglected needs, problem areas, and unique open doors ready for disturbance. This client driven approach fills in as a directing star, enlightening the way to significant development.

Embracing Disappointment As A Venturing Stone

The excursion to leading-edge thoughts is seldom straight. It's laden with disappointments, impasses, and premature moves. In any case, embracing disappointment as a vital piece of the cycle is a sign of imaginative masterminds. Disappointment isn't an endpoint, yet a venturing stone. Every disappointment offers significant experiences and examples that push trend-setters nearer to their definitive objective. The readiness to gain from disappointment, adjust, and continue on is which isolates the individuals who stagger from the people who take off.

Developing A Culture OF Development
Development isn't the consequence of a solitary splendid brain; it flourishes in a culture that sustains and upholds it. Associations that esteem advancement cultivate a climate where trial and error is empowered, risk-taking is embraced, and

different viewpoints are praised. Such societies focus on consistent learning, offer assets for imaginative investigation, and give stages to workers to contribute their thoughts, no matter their progressive position.

The Craft OF Thought Age

Thought age is both a workmanship and a science. Methods, for example, conceptualizing, mind planning, and converse reasoning can light the inventive flash, empowering creative answers to arise. Making places of refuge for thought age, where judgment is suspended and wild thoughts are invited, can prompt surprising leap forwards. Also, looking for motivation from irrelevant spaces, participating in freestyle investigation, and testing ordinary ideas can all animate the progression of new thoughts.

The Job Of Instinct

Instinct assumes a critical part in recognizing advancement thoughts. It's the psyche mind handling abundant data and encounters, introducing out-of-nowhere experiences. While judicious examination is fundamental, permitting instinct to direct the ideation interaction can prompt those "Aha!" minutes that steer development. Supporting instinct includes care, reflection, and attention to gut feelings.

Approval And Emphasis
When a cutting-edge thought is recognized, the excursion is nearly finished. Approval is an urgent move toward guaranteeing that the view tends to actual requirements and is practical. Input from clients, specialists, and partners refines the idea and shapes it into a serviceable arrangement. The course of emphasis - refining, testing, and developing the thought - is an iterative dance that changes a crude idea into a cleaned diamond.

Recognizing and developing advanced thoughts is the heartbeat of advancement. It's the most common way of inspiring bigger thoughts, of searching out new points of view, and of really considering testing the standard. The excursion is described by interest, flexibility, and readiness to gain from disappointments. As we embrace different points of view, break up limits, and encourage societies of advancement, we open the possibility to reshape ventures, improve lives, and move society forward. The way from zero to one is enlightened by the steady quest for leading-edge thoughts, and it's through this pursuit that we uncover the endless conceivable outcomes that lie ahead.

THREE

THE ART OF BUILDING A VISIONARY TEAM

In the unique development scene, fabricating a visionary group is a foundation of progress. A group's aggregate assets, different points of view, and shared responsibility can intensify the effect of cutting-edge thoughts, changing them into unmistakable fundamental factors. This investigation digs into the craft of collecting, supporting, and driving a visionary group. This group embraces development and pushes it forward through cooperation, mutual perspective, and steadfast commitment.

The Force OF Aggregate Virtuoso

A visionary group is more than the number of its singular individuals. It's a blend of different gifts, abilities, and encounters that, when consolidated, make a strong power fit for tackling complex issues and driving development. Each colleague brings a novel point of view, testing the standard way of thinking and pushing the limits of innovativeness. When outfit successfully, the aggregate virtuoso of a visionary group can prompt weighty forward leaps that change enterprises and society at large.

Shared Vision And Reason

At the core of a visionary group lies a common vision and reason. This shared objective fills in as a North Star, directing the group's endeavors and adjusting their activities. A convincing vision lights enthusiasm and responsibility, cultivating a feeling of solidarity that rises above individual jobs. At the point when a common perspective drives colleagues, they are bound to team up consistently, influence their assets, and work solidly towards understanding their aggregate goals.

Embracing Variety And Incorporation

Variety is a wellspring of development. A visionary group blossoms by incorporating people from different foundations, societies, and disciplines. This variety brings a variety of points of view that challenge suppositions and advance critical thinking. Consideration, then again, establishes a climate where each voice is esteemed, adding to a feeling of having a place that urges each colleague to share their one-of-a-kind experiences without a second thought.

Cultivating A Culture OF Trust

Trust is the bedrock after visionary groups are assembled. Colleagues should trust each other's mastery, aims, and obligation to the shared vision. A culture of trust engages colleagues to go ahead with reasonable plans of action, express their thoughts uninhibitedly, and offer productive input unafraid of judgment. This climate of mental well-being is fundamental for sustaining advancement, as it energizes trial and error and cultivates open exchange.

Corresponding Ranges Of Abilities

Building a visionary group requires a fragile equilibrium of ranges of abilities. While various capabilities are fundamental, it's similarly critical that colleagues' assets complete one another. A balanced group has a blend of specialized mastery, inventive reasoning, initiative keenness, and relational abilities. This cooperative energy permits the group to handle complex difficulties from various points, bringing about all-encompassing and innovative arrangements.

Administration That Rouses

A visionary group needs initiative that moves, guides and enables. A creative chief conveys the vision and establishes a climate where each colleague feels esteemed and spurred. A compassionate industry cultivates a culture of coordinated effort, energizes risk-taking, and offers the help essential for colleagues to release their maximum capacity. A pioneer who shows others how it's done embraces disappointment as a learning potential open door, and commends accomplishments that can motivate the group to arrive at new levels of development.

Powerful Correspondence And Coordinated Effort

Correspondence is the soul of a visionary group. Open, straightforward correspondence works with trading thoughts, advanced arrangement, and forestall errors. Ordinary registrations, meetings to generate new ideas, and gatherings for sharing advancement keep colleagues connected and informed. Cooperation apparatuses and stages can connect geological hindrances, empowering worldwide groups to team up flawlessly, regardless of their area.

Empowering Scholarly Contact
Advancement blossoms with sound discussion and scholarly rubbing. A visionary group urges colleagues to challenge each other's thoughts and presumptions. Conscious conflicts lead to more profound bits of knowledge and more powerful arrangements. Scholarly grinding flashes imaginative pressure that animates new points of view, eventually driving the group to investigate roads they probably won't have thought about.

Acknowledgment And Strengthening
Perceiving and enabling colleagues is urgent for cultivating a feeling of responsibility and

responsibility. Recognizing commitments, commending victories, and giving independence in navigation can improve camaraderie and inspiration. At the point when colleagues feel esteemed and engaged, they are bound to contribute their energy, imagination, and commitment to understanding the group's vision.

Nonstop Learning And Development
A visionary group doesn't become complacent but focuses on nonstop learning and development. Development requires remaining on top of things, embracing advances, and adjusting to developing business sector patterns. Empowering continuous expertise advancement, giving chances to educate broadly, and staying inquisitive is fundamental for keeping the group's aggregate information and abilities at the front of the development.

Building a visionary group is diverse craftsmanship that requests a profound comprehension of human elements, coordinated effort, and initiative. At the point when people with different qualities and shared values meet up under a binding together reason, they can catalyze development that rises above individual commitments. The specialty of building a visionary group depends on encouraging trust, embracing variety, sustaining a culture of action, and enabling colleagues to succeed. Gathering and supporting such a group makes way for transforming visionary thoughts into the real world, empowering the excursion from zero to one and then some.

FOUR

CRAFTING A WINNING BUSINESS STRATEGY: LESSONS FROM THE FIRST MILE

In the confounded business universe, a triumphant system can be the distinction between victory and blankness. Each effective undertaking starts its excursion with a solitary step, frequently called the "principal mile." This underlying stage is primary, establishing the vibe for the whole endeavor and laying the groundwork for future development. In this investigation, we dig into the specialty of making a triumphant business procedure, drawing illustrations from the vital first mile that can direct business visionaries, new businesses, and laid-out organizations on their way from zero to one.

The Meaning of the Principal Mile
The main mile of a business process is something other than a symbolic beginning; it's a plan for what's in store. Similarly, as the strong groundwork is essential to build a transcending high rise, a well-created procedure during the main mile is imperative for supportable development and achievement. During this stage, basic choices are made, and the direction of the business is outlined. The examples learned in the main mile echo through each resulting selection, making its importance vital.

Grasping the Scene

Before setting out on the excursion, understanding the landscape is fundamental. This includes careful statistical surveying to recognize patterns, holes, and valuable open doors. Business people should be personally familiar with the requirements of their interest group and the severe scene they are entering. A far-reaching comprehension of the landscape considers the detailing of a technique that profits from market experiences and addresses neglected needs.

Characterizing the Offer

At the core of a triumphant business methodology lies a convincing incentive. This is the novel value that the business brings to its clients, separating it from competitors. Motivation is beyond a slogan; the commitment to advantages and arrangements resonates with the ideal interest group. Making a solid offer requires adjusting the business' assets to client trouble spots, displaying why the item or administration is the perfect arrangement that anyone could hope to find.

Putting forth Clear Objectives and Targets
A triumphant business methodology is grounded in clear and feasible objectives. Business visionaries should characterize what they expect to accomplish in the short and long haul. These objectives should be explicit, quantifiable, achievable, significant, and time-bound (Savvy). Whether it's catching a specific portion of the overall industry, accomplishing an income achievement, or venturing into new locales, distinct objectives act as signals that guide the direction and focus on activities.

Adjusting to Input

In the main mile, organizations frequently work in strange areas, and gaining from encounters is basic. Business visionaries should be available for input, whether it's from clients, guides, or early adopters. Criticism acts as a rude awakening, uncovering vulnerable sides and highlighting regions that require improvement. The capacity to adjust and repeat in light of criticism indicates a robust and imaginative business methodology.

Development as a Foundation

Development isn't an extravagance; it's a need. A triumphant business methodology embraces development as a foundation. This could include problematic innovation, novel plans of action, or imaginative ways to tackle client trouble spots. Advancement isn't restricted to item improvement; it reaches out to showcase systems, client commitment, and functional effectiveness. By consistently looking for creative arrangements, organizations stay cutthroat and pertinent in a rapidly developing scene.

Building a Versatile Foundation

Development is an essential target for any business, and a triumphant methodology considers versatility all along. This includes building a foundation to deal with expanded requests, venture into new business sectors, and grow new items or administrations. Versatility has functional abilities and the adaptability to adjust to changing conditions without forfeiting quality or the client experience.

Developing Client Connections

The main mile is a fantastic chance to develop significant client connections that persevere. Beyond giving an item or administration, organizations should zero in on making meaningful encounters that encourage dedication and support. This includes undivided attention, customized connections, and a promise to tend to client needs expeditiously. Building solid client connections upgrades brand notoriety and frequently prompts informal exchanges of references, a strong development driver.

Adjusting present-moment and long-haul Objectives

A triumphant business system finds some harmony between momentary increases and long-haul vision. While prompt income generation is fundamental, it shouldn't come to the detriment of forfeiting the business' drawn-out potential. Business people should consider what their choices today will mean for their capacity to accomplish reasonable development and advancement later on. Adjusting present-moment and long-haul targets requires critical reasoning and a commitment to the master plan.

Exploring Difficulties with Versatility

Challenges are unavoidable in any business venture. The principal mile frequently presents unexpected snags that test a business visionary's strength and versatility. A triumphant business technique furnishes business visionaries with the outlook to see difficulties as any open doors for development. As opposed to being dissuaded by problems, versatile business visionaries gain from them, turn when fundamental, and use misfortune as an impetus for refining their system.

Embracing a Persistent Learning Society

The excursion from zero to one is a powerful cycle that requires steady learning and development. A triumphant business technique empowers a culture of constant advancement inside the association. Business visionaries should remain refreshed on industry patterns, client inclinations, and arising advances. Moreover, cultivating a culture where workers are urged to grow their abilities and contribute novel thoughts encourages a climate of development and versatility.

Observing Achievements and Progress
Praising achievements and progress is fundamental for confidence and inspiration. As the business accomplishes its objectives, both tiny and huge, it's critical to require the investment to recognize and praise these accomplishments. Perceiving progress lifts the group's confidence level and supports the arrangement between the methodology and the ideal results. Festivities act as tokens of the excursion's prosperity and fuel the drive

to arrive at significantly more noteworthy levels.

Making a triumphant business methodology is a workmanship that joins market understanding, development, versatility, and flexibility. The illustrations gained from the essential first mile establish the groundwork for future growth and achievement. By understanding the scene, characterizing a convincing offer, laying out clear objectives, and embracing input, business visionaries can fabricate a procedure that explores difficulties, drives development, and positions the business for the supported product. The excursion from zero to one is set apart by essential decisions that shape the company's direction, making a tradition of development, effect, and achievement.

FIVE

CREATING MONOPOLY: UNLEASHING THE POWER OF UNIQUE VALUE

In business, making syndication surpasses simple market predominance; offering an exceptional incentive successfully removes the contest. A syndication doesn't simply control a market; it characterizes it, setting the norm for what purchasers need and need. This investigation dives into the craft of making syndication by releasing the force of one-of-a-kind worth, exhibiting how organizations can shape enterprises, catch markets, and make a permanent imprint on the business scene.

Reclassifying Syndication

Generally, "syndication" has been related to the convergence of market power in possessing a solitary substance. Be that as it may, in the present unique business climate, making syndication doesn't guarantee smothering contests through legitimate or administrative means. It's tied in with accomplishing a degree of uniqueness and worth that contenders see as staggeringly challenging to recreate.

The Pith of Remarkable Worth

Making an imposing business model relies on offering an extraordinary worth that resounds profoundly with clients. This worth isn't just gradual; a distinct advantage addresses neglected needs, takes care of perplexing issues or improves the client experience in a way that hasn't been finished previously. This uniqueness separates a business, pursuing it as an objective of decision for shoppers who look for the unrivaled advantages it gives.

Development as an Impetus

Development is the fuel that drives the production of imposing business models. Organizations that make progress toward syndication don't become complacent; they consistently redefine known limits, embrace troublesome innovations and investigate new methodologies. Development fills in as a vehicle for conveying extraordinary worth, whether through leading-edge items, historic administrations, or groundbreaking action plans.

Understanding Client Wants

Making syndication includes personally figuring out the cravings and desires of clients. It's tied in with distinguishing trouble spots, challenges, and neglected needs that clients may not be completely mindful of. By digging into client conduct, inclinations, and input, organizations can foster contributions that fulfill current requirements and shape future assumptions.

The Quest for Greatness

Greatness isn't simply an objective; it's the foundation of making an imposing business model. Organizations that progress toward one-of-a-kind worth don't make do with unremarkableness; they seek greatness in each feature of their tasks. From item plan and assembling to client care and experience, each touchpoint mirrors a promise to convey excellent worth.

Bridling Organization Impacts

Network impacts assume a crucial part in making syndication. As a business draws in additional clients or clients, the worth of its contribution increments dramatically. The more individuals utilize an item or administration, the more critical it becomes to other people. This self-building cycle creates a temperate circle that hardens a business' situation and makes it progressively challenging for contenders to get up to speed.

Putting resources into Scholarly Capital

Scholarly capital is an essential resource chasing syndication. Organizations that put resources into innovative work, develop a culture of development, and safeguard their licensed innovation make obstructions to sections that dissuade likely contenders.

Scholarly capital encourages the production of one-of-a-kind worth and shields it, making replication an overwhelming errand for other people.

Vital Associations and Biological Systems
Making restraining infrastructure frequently includes fashioning vital associations and environments that enhance the offer. Joint efforts with integral organizations or innovations can grow the scope and effect of an item or administration. By coordinating flawlessly with the existence of clients through organizations, a business sets its situation as a fundamental piece of its environment.

The Job of Marking and Notoriety
A solid brand and notoriety are fundamental for making restraining infrastructure. Clients ought to connect the business with quality, dependability, and dependability. A strong

standing draws in new clients and holds existing ones, encouraging dedication and backing that can be trying for contenders to recreate.

Risk-Taking and the Drawn-out View
Making syndication requires a readiness to proceed with carefully weighed-out courses of action and embrace a drawn-out point of view. Organizations should put resources into advancement, and emphasize thoughts and climate misfortunes in the quest for extraordinary worth. This obligation to the big-picture approach frequently implies persevering through momentary difficulties to commit to long-haul strength.

The Test of Supporting Uniqueness
Keeping an imposing business model isn't without its difficulties. As a business lays out a predominant position, contenders will, without a doubt, endeavor to imitate its

prosperity. Supporting uniqueness requires consistent carefulness, proceeding with development, and a determined spotlight on client needs. Organizations become a complacent gamble, losing the very uniqueness that put them aside.
The Moral Aspect

While the quest for imposing a business model can drive development and wealth creation, it likewise raises moral contemplations. Organizations should adjust their pursuit of exceptional worth with a more extensive effect on purchasers, contenders, and society at large. Guaranteeing that restraining infrastructure doesn't prompt unreasonable practices or obstruct sound contests is fundamental for cultivating a supportable business scene.

Making an imposing business model is an excursion that rises above conventional ideas of market strength. Offering extraordinary worth resounds with clients, characterizes enterprises, and sets new norms. The quest for interesting worth drives development cultivates greatness, and lights a pledge to convey unrivaled advantages. Organizations that prevail regarding making syndication leave through inheritance, molding markets, catching purchaser reliability, and making a permanent imprint on the business scene into the indefinite future.

SIX

THE STARTUP MINDSET: EMBRACING UNCERTAINTY AND RISK

In business, the startup outlook is a power that compels people to transform dreams into the real world, thoughts into items, and vulnerabilities into valuable open doors. It's a mentality set apart by daringness, versatility, and an eagerness to explore unfamiliar waters. At the core of this outlook lies the hug of vulnerability and chance - twin mates on the excursion from zero to one. This investigation dives into the substance of the startup mentality, revealing insight into how embracing vulnerability and hazard becomes the foundation of extraordinary development and achievement.

The Underpinning of Development

At its center, the startup outlook flourishes with development. It's the opposite of smugness, driven by a longing for change and improvement. Business people with this outlook aren't happy with the state of affairs; they are consumed by the need to challenge standards, upset ventures, and achieve positive change. This voracious hunger for advancement energizes the boldness to step into the obscure and tackle the force of vulnerability.

The Idea of Vulnerability
Vulnerability is the texture of business. New companies set out on an excursion with restricted data, exploring strange regions where results are rarely ensured. The startup outlook doesn't avoid vulnerability; all things being equal, it inclines toward it, regarding it as a material after that to paint prospects. Embracing vulnerability implies recognizing the potential for disappointment while declining to be deadened by it.

Risk as an Impetus for Development

Risk is the other side of the innovative coin. The startup outlook doesn't fear risk; it uses it as an impetus for development. Well balanced plan of action taking is a principal trait of this outlook. Business visionaries gauge the likely prizes against the dangers, and when the potential for remuneration offsets the chance of disappointment, they jump. Risk is the money of progress, and the startup mentality comprehends that advancement frequently requires getting out of a safe place.

Learning Through Trial and Error

The startup mentality embraces trial and error for learning. Business visionaries perceive that the way to progress is cleared with disappointments, misfortunes, and surprising difficulties. Instead of reviewing disappointments as barriers, they view them as venturing stones toward understanding what works and doesn't. Trial and error permits business visionaries to test presumptions, accumulate information, and turn when essential while crawling more like a feasible arrangement.

Adjusting to Change

Change is a steady friend of the pioneering venture. Markets develop, client inclinations shift, and mechanical progressions reshape scenes. The startup outlook embraces change as an open door instead of a danger. Business visionaries with this mentality are deft and prepared to turn their procedures and change their course founded on new data. Versatility signifies progress, permitting new businesses to stay pertinent and cutthroat in unique conditions.

Flexibility Even with Misfortunes

Flexibility is a principal quality of the startup outlook. The innovative excursion is laden with difficulties, misfortunes, and snapshots of self-question. Be that as it may, the startup attitude doesn't flounder in that frame of mind of trouble; it bounces back with significantly more noteworthy assurance. Business people view disappointments as transitory road obstructions, not long-lasting losses. This versatility keeps them on the way to development in any event when the street appears to be deceptive.

The Mentality of Cleverness
New companies frequently work with restricted assets, constraining business people from embracing a mentality of creativity. The startup mentality tracks down imaginative ways of achieving objectives, utilizing accessible resources, and investigating flighty arrangements. This cleverness encourages development, pushing business visionaries to

consider new ideas and find open doors where others see hindrances.

Long Haul Vision During Momentary Difficulties

While new companies might confront momentary difficulties, the startup outlook keeps a drawn-out vision. Business visionaries comprehend that achievement is an excursion, and difficulties are simple blips on the radar. A drawn-out picture gives the fundamental point of view to get through quick difficulties, zeroing in on a definitive objective of making extraordinary effects.

Building an Organization of Help

The startup outlook perceives the significance of an encouraging group of people. Business people encircle themselves with coaches, counselors, and friends who offer direction, knowledge, and a security net during testing times. An organization of help gives different points of view, a sounding board for thoughts, and a wellspring of consolation that energizes the pioneering soul.

The Harmony between Desire and Authenticity

The startup mentality finds some harmony between aspiration and authenticity. While business visionaries think ambitiously and imagine extraordinary results, they ground their yearnings truly. Desire drives them to try the impossible, yet authenticity keeps their feet immovably established on the ground, guaranteeing that objectives are reachable and progress is quantifiable.

The startup outlook combines boldness, strength, development, and chance-taking. A perspective flourishes in vulnerability, finding open doors where others see difficulties. Embracing exposure and hazard

is the backbone of this outlook, impelling
business people to manufacture new ways,
disturb ventures, and leave behind a legacy.
With the startup attitude as their compass,
business people explore the unknown waters
of business with faithful assurance and an
unshakeable obligation to change their
dreams into fundamental factors.

SEVEN

MARKETING FOR THE FUTURE: CAPTURING HEARTS AND MINDS

In a quickly developing business scene,
promoting plays rose above conventional
parts. It became a unique power that shapes
discernments, impacts ways of behaving, and
catches the hearts and psyches of purchasers.
As innovation advances and purchaser
assumptions develop, the craft of promoting

should adjust to stay pertinent and viable. This investigation digs into the procedures and rules that characterize promoting the future, zeroing in on the art of catching hearts and brains in a world described by steady change and development.

The Shift Toward Relationship-Driven Promoting

Promoting what's in store is set apart by a shift from value-based ways to deal with relationship-driven procedures. Buyers today look for credible associations with brands that align with their qualities and goals. Effective showcasing goes past advancing items; it recounts a convincing story that resounds with shoppers on a more profound level. Building enduring connections through trust and shared values becomes a foundation of future-centered showcasing.

Profound Reverberation: The Way to Catching Hearts

Catching hearts requires close-to-home reverberation. Future-situated advertising inspires feelings that reverberate with customers' yearnings, wants, and encounters. Brands that tap into emotions like delight, sympathy, or wistfulness make vital associations that wait for customers long after the advertising message is conveyed. Close-to-home reverberation goes past highlights and advantages, creating a bond that perseveres through time.

Narrating as a Vehicle of Association

Narrating arises as a powerful device in the advertiser's weapons store. Brands that art convincing stories bring purchasers into an existence where they can connect with characters, difficulties, and wins. Stories construct compassion, inspire feelings, and give a setting to customers to see themselves inside the brand's excursion. Story-driven advertising changes messages into encounters that reverberate and lock in.

Personalization in a Hyper-Associated World

Personalization becomes the overwhelming focus in advertising for what's to come. Hyper-associated buyers expect fitted encounters that take special care of their one-of-a-kind inclinations and requirements. High-level information examination and manufactured intelligence-driven knowledge empowers brands to convey customized content, proposals, and offers. This individual touch catches consideration and develops a feeling of being perceived and esteemed by the brand.

Intelligent Commitment and Cooperation

Advertising for what's to come blossoms with intuitive commitment. Brands that welcome shoppers to effectively take an interest, contribute, and co-make encounters produce further associations. Intelligent components, for example, client-created content, surveys, tests, and challenges, energize commitment and fabricate a feeling of the local area around the brand. This participatory methodology changes uninvolved shoppers into dynamic supporters.

Maintainability and Social Obligation

The future-cognizant purchaser values maintainability and social obligation. Brands that align with these qualities catch hearts by showing their duty to have a constructive outcome on society and the climate. Promoting methodologies that feature supportable practices, moral obtaining, and local area commitment resound with

purchasers who focus on conscious
utilization.

Consistent Omni-Channel Encounters

The eventual fate of advertising is described
via consistent omnichannel encounters.
Shoppers move smoothly across different
touchpoints, from virtual entertainment
stages to online business sites, actual stores,
to portable applications. Consistency and
cognizance in informing, marking, and client
experience across these channels make a
bound together brand character and improve
purchaser trust.

Legitimacy in the Time of Straightforwardness

Legitimacy is vital in promoting what's to
come. Customers know and request
straightforwardness from brands. Showcasing
veritable, honest messages that line up with
the brand's activities assemble believability

and encourage trust. Brands that are credible in their correspondence and associations make significant associations that go the distance.

Adjusting to Arising Innovations

Advertising for what's to come embraces arising innovations to connect with and enrapture crowds. Computer-generated reality (VR), expanded reality (AR), manufactured consciousness (simulated intelligence), and vivid encounters reclassify how brands communicate with buyers. Brands that integrate these innovations into their systems make noteworthy minutes that have an enduring effect.

Reason Driven Marking

Reason-driven marking reverberates profoundly with customers looking for brands that align with their qualities. Brands that lucid an unmistakable reason past benefit exhibit a pledge to having a beneficial outcome on society. Reason-driven promoting catches the hearts and conventions of purchasers around a common defense, transforming them into steadfast backers.

Measurements Past Numbers: Estimating Profound Effect

Estimating the outcome of showcasing what's in store goes past customary measurements. While snaps, changes, and commitment rates stay significant, the close-to-home effect becomes a fundamental measure. Brands evaluate how well their advertising efforts summon feelings, motivate activity, and cultivate associations. Catching hearts and psyches is reflected in the profound reverberation of the brand's information.

Building a Local area of Supporters
Showcasing for what's in store shifts from one-way correspondence to building a local area of backers. Brands that cultivate a feeling of having a place and urge customers to share their encounters make an organization of steadfast allies. Verbal exchange showcasing from enthusiastic backers holds an unmatched impact in catching the hearts and psyches of new customers.

Showcasing for what's to come rises above customary limits, transforming into an influential power that catches hearts and psyches. It's an essential mix of profound reverberation, customized encounters, genuineness, reason-driven stories, and state-of-the-art innovations. Brands that ace this craftsmanship make associations that rise above exchanges, transforming buyers into steadfast supporters who champion the brand's main goal and values. As the business scene develops, showcasing what's in store demonstrates the force of advancement, sympathy, and human association.

EIGHT

SCALING WITH PURPOSE: GROWING WITHOUT LOSING YOUR IDENTITY

In the excursion of a business venture, scaling a business is often seen as the sacred goal of progress. Even so, the road to development is filled with difficulties, and one of the main worries is keeping up with the embodiment of the business as it extends. Scaling with objects is craftsmanship, including developing the business while safeguarding its fundamental beliefs, character, and uniqueness. This investigation dives into the methodologies and rules that guide business people in scaling without losing their personality, guaranteeing that their spirit stays in one piece as the business develops.

Characterizing the Substance

Before leaving on the excursion of scaling, characterizing the embodiment of the business is fundamental. What values, convictions, and standards support the organization's tasks? What separates the company from its rivals? Characterizing the pith gives a compass that guides navigation, guaranteeing that development lines up with the center personality.

Developing Areas of strength for a Culture
Culture is the core of a business' character. As a business scales, supporting areas of strength become considerably more essential. A culture that underlines coordinated effort, development, straightforwardness, and shared values goes about as a bringing together power. Regardless of their job, each worker adds to the way of life, forming the business' character through their activities and associations.

Adjusting Development to Values
Scaling with reason includes adjusting development drives to the organization's qualities. Each essential choice, from recruiting new workers to venturing into new

business sectors, ought to mirror the qualities that characterize the business. This arrangement guarantees that development only thinks about the respectability of the business's personality.

Straightforwardness in Correspondence

Keeping a feeling of character during development requires straightforward correspondence. Workers, clients, and partners must comprehend the explanations for development endeavors and how they interface with the business' fundamental beliefs. A concise post encourages trust and guarantees that everybody agrees as the business scales.

Enabling Authority

Strengthening is critical to scaling with reason. Pioneers who engage their groups to decide, develop, and add to the business' development establish a climate where the personality can thrive. Enabled groups are bound to maintain the organization's qualities and vision as they effectively form its future.

Consolidating Criticism

Paying attention to criticism from representatives, clients, and different partners is fundamental to keeping up with personality during development. Input gives experiences into how the business' extension endeavors are seen and whether they align with the central character's assumptions. Consolidating information considers course adjustments and guarantees that development endeavors stay doing great.

Adjusting Worldwide and Neighborhood

As a business scales, it might venture into new locales or markets. Offsetting a worldwide presence with neighborhood pertinence is fundamental for saving the business' character. While the guiding principle stays predictable, adjusting to nearby societies, inclinations, and subtleties exhibits a promise of understanding and serving different crowds.

Focusing on Client Experience
A business' personality is frequently intently attached to the encounters it offers clients. As the company develops, focusing on client experience becomes vital. Each communication ought to mirror the brand's personality and values, making a reliable encounter that clients can depend on, regardless of the business' size.

Particular Development Techniques

Scaling with reason includes being particular in development techniques. Not all potential open doors align with the business' character or values. Business visionaries must survey imaginable development ways and pick those reverberating to the company's substance. Particular development guarantees that the industry extends in a manner that builds up its personality instead of weakening it.

Safeguarding Pioneer's Vision
The vision of the organizer frequently shapes a business' personality. As the business scales, safeguarding the organizer's dream becomes a method for respecting its underlying foundations. Pioneers can remain effectively associated with directing development, guaranteeing that the organization's advancement remains consistent with the first aim.

Cultivating Development

Advancement is fundamental for scaling with reason. It's tied in with tracking down imaginative ways of growing while at the same time remaining consistent with the business's personality. Creative methodologies permit the company to develop while holding uniqueness, and the components reverberate with clients.

Keeping away from the Enticement of Congruity
Chasing development, organizations might be enticed to adjust to industry standards or patterns. Be that as it may, scaling with reason implies opposing this allurement. While it's critical to stay versatile, changing to designs that don't match the business' character gambles weakens its uniqueness.

Persistent Reflection and Transformation

Scaling with objects is a continuous cycle that requires consistent reflection and variation. Business people need to intermittently evaluate the development direction and guarantee that it stays aligned with its character and values. Reflection prompts course amendments and changes on a case-by-case basis.

Scaling with design is a multifaceted dance that requires a fragile harmony between development and character. As organizations extend, the test lies in guaranteeing that development endeavors maintain the guiding principle, convictions, and uniqueness that characterize the organization's personality. The craft of scaling without losing character includes:
Supporting society.
Adjusting development to values.
Pursuing vital choices that mirror the substance of the business.

By embracing reason-driven development, business visionaries can accomplish extension while safeguarding the spirit of their business, guaranteeing that as the business advances, its character stays immovable and valid.

NINE

INNOVATION BEYOND THE HORIZON: SUSTAINING SUCCESS IN CHANGING LANDSCAPES

Advancement has been the main impetus behind progress, driving social orders and businesses forward. In any case, in the present, quickly impacting the world, the development skyline reaches beyond simple mechanical progressions. Supporting progress in unique scenes requests a proactive and versatile methodology that envelops historical thoughts and the capacity to explore moving standards. This investigation dives into the procedures and rules that guide organizations and people in advancing into the great beyond, guaranteeing that achievement perseveres during evolving tides.

Reclassifying Advancement

Advancement is not generally bound to new devices or troublesome innovations. It incorporates a comprehensive way to deal with critical thinking, enveloping new plans of action, novel techniques, and groundbreaking perspectives. Organizations and people should reclassify advancement to incorporate versatility, flexibility, and the ability to flourish in questionable landscapes.

Embracing Vagueness

The outcome of changing scenes requires embracing uncertainty. What's in store is erratic, and the capacity to explore through vulnerability becomes an upper hand. The individuals who embrace uncertainty as an open door instead of danger are better prepared to expect shifts, answer really, and quickly jump over arising chances.

Developing a Learning Mentality

A learning mentality is the bedrock of development into the great beyond. This mentality includes a pledge to consistent growth, an eagerness to challenge suppositions, and a receptiveness to new viewpoints. People and organizations that develop a learning outlook adjust promptly to change and are more receptive to arising patterns.

Dexterous Advancement Systems

Lithe development systems give an organized way to deal with adjusting in evolving scenes. Ideas like Plan Thinking, Lean Startup, and Lithe procedures work with iterative critical thinking, quick trial and error, and constant input circles. These systems empower organizations to turn quickly because of market shifts.

Encouraging a Culture of Development
Supporting achievement requires a culture that qualities and sustains development. Organizations must establish a climate where workers are urged to think imaginatively, challenge standards, and contribute their thoughts. A culture of development enables groups to embrace change, explore boldly, and adjust their techniques when required.

Utilizing Innovation and Mechanization
Innovation assumes a critical part in development into the great beyond. Mechanization, computerized reasoning, and information investigation empower organizations to smooth out processes, improve client encounters, and uncover bits of knowledge that guide independent direction. Utilizing innovation guarantees

that development is implanted into each part of the business.

Client Driven Development

In a quickly evolving scene, client inclinations and ways of behaving develop soon. Client-driven development includes remaining sensitive to these movements and consistently adjusting items, administrations, and encounters to address advancing issues. Organizations that focus on the client experience and integrate input into their procedures are bound to support achievement.

Variety and Cooperation

Variety energizes development by uniting a scope of points of view, encounters, and thoughts. Cooperative conditions that energize cross-practical groups and interdisciplinary joint efforts encourage a fruitful ground for inventive reasoning.

Various groups are better prepared to expect change and devise multi-layered arrangements.

Risk-Taking and Versatility

Development into the great beyond implies determined risk-taking and versatility. It's tied in with recognizing that disappointment is a likely result; however, embracing it as a venturing stone toward progress. A readiness to face challenges and the capacity to return from difficulties empowers organizations and people to weather conditions and storms and become more grounded.

Long Haul Vision in a Transient World

Supporting achievement requires a drawn-out vision in a world frequently centered around transient additions. Organizations that focus on long-haul objectives over quick satisfaction are better situated to pursue vital choices that align with their fundamental beliefs and future desires.

Ecological and Social Obligation
Advancement should reach out to past benefits to envelop natural and social obligations. Organizations that consider the more extensive effect of their activities are bound to explore moving scenes effectively. Economic practices and a promise to moral lead reverberate with customers and add to long-haul achievement.

Versatile Administration
Authority in unique scenes requests versatility. Pioneers who rouse, guide, and engage their groups establish a climate that flourishes with development. Versatile pioneers expect change, impart successfully, and encourage a feeling of direction that

inspires people to contribute their brightest thoughts.

Remaining Inquisitive and Liberal

Interest and liberality are fundamental attributes for development into the great beyond. Remaining inquisitive prompts people and organizations to look for new data, investigate arising patterns and challenge existing suspicions. A receptive outlook considers joining assorted points of view that can prompt advancement thoughts.

Vital Associations and Biological Systems

Exploring changing scenes frequently includes teaming up with critical accomplices and partaking in environments. Associations empower organizations to use correlative qualities and extend their compass. Settings give valuable chances to systems administration, information sharing, and cross-industry development.

Advancement into the great beyond rises above customary limits and regular definitions. It's tied in with embracing change, developing a learning mentality, and building versatile systems that support progress in unique scenes. The craft of advancement includes staying open to arising conceivable outcomes, rocking the boat, and utilizing innovation, variety, and coordinated effort. By rethinking development to envelop flexibility, agility, and long-haul vision, people and organizations can flourish amid vulnerability, which is imaginative and enduringly fruitful to create a future.

TEN

ETHICS IN ENTREPRENEURSHIP: NAVIGATING MORAL DILEMMAS

The business venture is often celebrated as a domain of development, risk-taking, and development. In any case, a mind-boggling scene of moral issues and contemplations is underneath the surface. Adjusting the quest for benefit with moral standards is a test that business people face consistently. Exploring these ethical difficulties isn't only fundamental for building a fruitful business and contributing decidedly to society. This investigation digs into the meaning of morals in business ventures. It gives bits of knowledge into how business visionaries can explore moral predicaments while making organizations stand on areas of strength for an establishment.

The Moral Goal
Morals are the ethical compass that guides independent direction and conduct. In business, morals reach out past private convictions; they shape the effect of organizations on partners, the climate, and society overall. Business visionaries use impact and power, and with that power comes liability. Maintaining moral principles

isn't simply a question of decision; guaranteeing a business's drawn-out maintainability and validity is a goal.

The Ethical Difficulties of Business

Business people frequently experience moral predicaments that challenge their qualities and standards. These difficulties can go from choices about valuing, advertising, and organizations to issues concerning worker treatment, ecological effect, and social obligation. Finding harmony between benefit-driven objectives and moral contemplations can be complicated, requiring cautious thought and reflection.

Straightforwardness and Genuineness

Straightforwardness and genuineness structure the bedrock of moral business ventures. Business people are liable for guaranteeing that their partners, including clients, representatives, financial backers, and accomplices, approach precise and honest data. Misdirecting or tricky practices dissolve the trust and harm a business' standing.

Adjusting Benefit and Reason

The deep-rooted discussion of benefit versus intention is vital to moral business. Business visionaries should consider whether their strategic approaches align with their overall objectives. Taking a stab at an advantage is normal, yet when it comes to the detriment of moral standards, the drawn-out results can offset momentary increases.

Natural and Social Obligation

Moral business venture goes past financial additions to include ecological and social obligations. Business visionaries ought to evaluate the effect of their procedure on the climate and society. Embracing economic works, limiting waste, and rewarding the local area add to a positive moral picture.

Fair Treatment of Representatives

Representatives are fundamental partners in any business. Moral treatment of representatives includes fair wages, safe working circumstances, equivalent open doors, and a steady workplace. Organizations that focus on the prosperity and development of their representatives make a culture of moral business.

Staying away from Shifty Practices

Business visionaries should be careful about avoiding manipulative practices, particularly in supply chains. From obtaining unrefined components to collaborating with providers, organizations should guarantee that their tasks don't add to manipulative work practices or infringement on fundamental freedoms.

Morals in Promoting and Publicizing

Promoting and publicizing raise moral worries when using tricky strategies, controlling feelings, or targeting weak socioeconomics. Moral showcasing includes straightforwardness, precision, and conveying items and administrations aligning with the commitments.

Moral Dynamic Structures

Exploring moral problems requires a precise methodology. Ethical dynamic systems, like utilitarianism, deontology, and righteous morals, give an organized method for examining moral contemplations and deciding the best strategy. These systems assist business visionaries with adjusting contending interests and settling on choices that line up with their qualities.

Making a Qualities-Driven Culture

Business visionaries can shape the way of life of their organizations. Developing a qualities-driven culture includes laying out moral rules, cultivating open correspondence, and empowering workers to voice worries unafraid of backlash. A culture that focuses on morals prompts a more durable and spurred labor force.

Long haul Outcomes of Moral Failures

Moral slips can have serious long-haul ramifications for organizations. A discolored standing, loss of client trust, lawful results, and adverse consequences on worker spirit are only a few likely results. Business visionaries should consider the possible aftermath of moral breaks before deciding.

Looking for Moral Counsel

Business visionaries can explore moral situations with others. Looking for direction from honest counselors, tutors, and industry specialists can give meaningful experiences and viewpoints. Working with individuals who focus on morals can assist business people with pursuing more educated choices.

Straightforwardness in Navigation

Moral navigation should be straightforward inside the association. Imparting the reasoning behind choices, even troublesome ones, encourages a culture of responsibility and trust. Straightforwardness likewise permits representatives to grasp the moral contemplations that guide the business.

Remaining Focused on Moral Advancement

Morals in a business venture aren't static; it develops close to the business and its working climate. Business visionaries should be available to adjust their moral standards as conditions change. Adaptability and a pledge to nonstop improvement are critical.

Morals in a business venture are not optional; a significant point of support characterizes the person and direction of a business. Exploring moral predicaments requires a sensitive harmony between benefits and standards. Business visionaries who focus on straightforwardness, decency, ecological obligation, and moral direction make organizations that stand as guides of trustworthiness in a constantly evolving scene. By installing moral contemplations into each part of their tasks, business visionaries add to a more honest and feasible business world that rises above prompt gains and holds back nothing.

CONCLUSION

EMPOWERING THE NEXT GENERATION OF VISIONARIES

As we ponder the sweeping excursion through the different components of business venture, development, morals, and development, it becomes clear that the enterprising soul is more than a business pursuit — an extraordinary power shapes economies, societies, and the actual structure holding the system together. From the commencement of earth-shattering plans to the route of moral situations, from scaling with reason to making manageable worth, this investigation has given an extensive look into the perplexing embroidery of the pioneering scene.

The scene of business venture is one of consistent development, directed by the persevering quest for new skylines. The stories of progress are entwined with tales of versatility, transformation, and an endless drive to make positive change. The accounts of visionaries who thought for even a second to resist show and champion imaginative arrangements exhibit the limit of human inventiveness to conquer difficulties and enlighten unfamiliar pathways.

In the sections devoted to advancement, we've seen the introduction of progressive ideas and the procedures that propel them from ideation to acknowledgment. The force of solitary reasoning, advancement thoughts, and visionary groups have enlightened the embodiment of development as a unique power that reshapes ventures and drives progress.

We've investigated the specialty of making visionary groups, understanding that achievement isn't simply the consequence of individual splendor but an aggregate exertion filled by variety, cooperation, and a shared obligation to understand a common vision. Trust, correspondence, and enthusiasm for greatness are the mind-boggling strings that tight-spot these groups together.

Scaling with reason arose as a focal topic, highlighting the meaning of capable development that keeps a business' character, values, and uprightness. Scaling isn't just about numbers; it's tied in with keeping a feeling of direction and credibility in a universe of evolving scenes. The techniques for making a triumphant business methodology showed that development is an incredible asset in creating an upper hand and holding onto the main mile.

Making restraining infrastructure grandstands how organizations can shape enterprises, reclassify showcases, and dazzle shoppers by offering exceptional worth that rises above rivalry. The quest for syndication requires a guarantee of development, key organizations, and a determined mission for greatness.

Development into the great beyond highlights that the innovative excursion isn't bound to spearhead items or administrations yet stretches out to cultivating a learning mentality, adjusting to change, and embracing a comprehensive way to deal with critical thinking. It's tied in with perceiving that advancement isn't an ultimate objective but a continuous undertaking that blossoms with interest and flexibility.

Morals in business ventures help us that the pursuit to remember achievement should be secured in rules that focus on straightforwardness, genuineness, and obligation. The ethical predicaments that business visionaries face highlight the requirement for moral dynamic systems, a qualities-driven culture, and a guarantee to make positive effects past monetary benefits.

In the consistently developing promoting scene, we've found that catching hearts and psyches includes winding around convincing accounts, embracing personalization, and utilizing innovation while staying unfaltering in credibility and straightforwardness.

Eventually, the pioneering venture is still in detachment. An excursion influences networks, impacts economies, and shapes the world. Engaging the up-and-coming age of visionaries includes passing on examples of development, morals, and capable development. It includes supporting a culture that cultivates inventiveness, embraces variety, and champions the quest for greatness.

As the mallet is given, starting with one age of visionaries and then onto the next, the business tradition keeps on unfurling, directed by similar persevering through upsides of resourcefulness, assurance, and the steadfast conviction that positive change is achievable. An inheritance spans limits, resists restrictions, and welcomes people in the future to rethink what's conceivable.

The enterprising soul flourishes in meeting rooms and new companies, however, in the hearts and psyches of people who hope against hope, advance, and change. The enterprising excursion is a tribute to human potential — demonstrating our capacity to shape the world and persevere through effect. As we engage the up-and-coming age of visionaries, let us recall that the journey for progress is unfathomable, and the skylines of business ventures are restricted exclusively by the extent of our creative mind and the profundity of our assurance.